Growing up in
CHRISTIANITY

Jean Holm and Romie Ridley

Series editor: Jean Holm

What is this book about?

One of the most interesting ways to learn about a religion is to try to see it through the eyes of children who are growing up in a religious family. In this way we can discover something of what it *feels* like to belong to the religion.

In the books in this series we shall be finding out how children gradually come to understand the real meaning of the festivals they celebrate, the scriptures and other stories they hear, the ceremonies they take part in, the symbols of their religion and the customs and traditions of their religious community. This should provide a good foundation for going on to a wider study of the religions.

The five books in this series deal with the main religions that are found in Britain today: Christianity, Hinduism, Islam, Judaism and Sikhism. However, some things are more important in one religion than in another. For example, festivals play a bigger part in the lives of Jewish children than they do in the lives of Sikh children, and the scriptures play a bigger part in the lives of Muslim children than they do in the lives of Hindu children, so although many of the same topics are dealt with in all the books, the pattern of each book is slightly different.

There are differences within every religion as well as between religions, and even a very long book could not describe the customs and beliefs of all the groups that make up a religion. In these books we may be learning more about one of the groups, or traditions, within the religion, but there will be references to the different ways in which other groups practise their faith.

In this series of books we are using BCE (Before the Christian Era) and CE (in the Christian Era) instead of BC and AD, which refer to Christian beliefs about the significance of Jesus.

How to use this book

Some of you will be studying religions for the first time. Others may already have learnt something about places of worship or festivals, and you will be able to gain greater understanding and fit what you know into a wider picture of the religion.

As you learn about how children grow up in a religion, prepare a display, or perhaps make a large class book. You will find some suggestions of activities in the text, but you will be able to think of many more. If your display is good enough it might be possible to put it up in the hall or in a corridor so that lots of people can see it. Try to show what it feels like to be on the 'inside' of the religion, so that other pupils and teachers and visitors to the school will be able to learn about the religion from the point of view of the children who are growing up in it.

Contents

Belonging   4

Being baptised   4
Being confirmed   10
Feeling you belong   12
Holy Communion   15
Taking part with the adults   20
Belonging to a world-wide Church   22
Belonging to a world religion   25
Pilgrimage   26

Times and seasons   30

Celebrating Christmas   30
Celebrating Easter   32
Holy Week   35
Round the Christian year   38

Learning about the faith   44

Learning at home   44
Learning with others   48
Meeting the Bible   52
Links with the past   54
Understanding beliefs   56
Growing in the faith   60

Glossary   62
Index   63

The words in the glossary are printed in **bold** the first time they appear in the book.

Belonging

Being baptised

"I was baptised as a baby. I have two godfathers and one godmother."

"In Mexico baptism in the Catholic Church is done almost immediately after the child is born. I saw both my brothers baptised. People are invited to the baptism. It's not planned, because the baby's born and the baptism's the next day, so it's not like a big ceremony. But all the relatives try to go."

> Baptism is one of the Christian 'rites of passage'. Rites of passage are ceremonies which mark important times in a person's life, the ending of one stage and the beginning of another. The main rites of passage are birth, initiation, marriage and death.

For Christians, baptism is 'initiation'. It marks a person's entry into the community of the Church. If the person who is being baptised is old enough to understand, the priest may say:

'Ruth, when you are baptized, you become a member of a new family. God takes you for his own child, and all Christian people will be your brothers and sisters.'

(From the Church of England *Alternative Service Book*)

In many Anglican churches, baptisms take place during one of the church services on Sunday, and the children in the congregation are invited to go and stand round the font so that they can see what is happening. During the service the priest makes the sign of the cross on the person's forehead, and says, 'I sign you with the cross, the sign of Christ. Do not be ashamed to confess the faith of Christ crucified'.

"We wanted our little girl to be baptised when she was a baby. I know she couldn't understand what was happening, but her godparents made the promises on her behalf. It was a lovely service. We were given candles to hold. Then after she had been baptised the vicar took us right up to the front, to stand facing the congregation."

A baby is baptised by an Anglican woman deacon.

When a lighted candle is given the priest says,

> 'Receive this light.
> This is to show that you have passed from darkness to light.'

and the congregation says,

> 'Shine as a light in the world to the glory of God the Father.'

Welcomed

When the newly baptised person is welcomed, the priest says,

> 'God has received you by baptism into his Church.'

and the congregation then says,

> 'We welcome you into the Lord's Family.
> We are members together of the body of Christ;
> We are children of the same heavenly Father;
> We are inheritors together of the kingdom of God.
> We welcome you.'   (*Alternative Service Book*)

Godparents are usually friends or relatives of the family. They promise to help and encourage their godchild to grow up as a Christian. It has become a custom for girls to have two godmothers and one godfather, and for boys to have two godfathers and one godmother.

> In the New Testament you can find Paul's description of the Church as the body of Christ, and baptism as the way in which Christians become members of the Church, in 1 Corinthians 12.12–13, 27.

"When our son was born we wanted to follow the Baptist Church pattern and so he was dedicated at about six months old. But when our daughter was born we were in Africa and we thought that it would be right for her to be baptised as we were part of the Anglican church as missionaries there. So our son was baptised as well. At the service the Bishop spoke in the local language and then translated it into English so that my parents, who were visiting us, could understand. The next day when we went for a walk two ladies came to the gate of their garden and said, 'These children are our children now; your children belong to the Church in Rwanda'. Only then did we realise just how important it was to the Christians and the church in Rwanda that we had them baptised there."

Different Churches have different customs. This person belongs to the Greek Orthodox Church (for the Orthodox Churches → page 24).

"For its baptism the baby is completely naked. They are plunged right under the water – three times, as the priest says 'The servant of God, Elisabeth, is baptised into the Name of the Father, Amen. And of the Son, Amen. And of the Holy Spirit, Amen.' In Greek, of course. Then water is splashed over their heads, and they are blessed. You get some horrendous screams sometimes! But everyone expects that the baby is going to cry. The priest always knows what to do, and the godparents know how to deal with it."

Christian names

Baptism is also a naming ceremony. The parents will have used the baby's name before the baptism, but during the ceremony the baby is given its 'Christian' names. The person who is conducting the service asks what the name is and then uses it like this: 'Michael James, I baptise you in the name of the Father, and of the Son, and of the Holy Spirit', and pours water on the baby's head.

1 Another name for Baptism is Christening. Sometimes it is called 'Christianing'. From this chapter and any other resources make a list of all the things involved in Baptism which show that someone is being 'Christianed'.

2 Begin a collection of Christian symbols and symbolic actions. Add to your collection as you go through this book.

A Greek Orthodox baptism.

Believers' Baptism

Most Christians are baptised when they are babies, but many Christians practise what is called 'Believers' Baptism'.

"In the Baptist church we have a dedication service to give thanks when the baby is born, and then when people are older they can be baptised. I was sixteen when I was baptised. In my baptismal class there were six or seven of us. There was one lady in her forties down to two who were younger than me. Week by week we went through the Baptismal so that we all understood what was going on and why we were doing it, and whether we felt ready because it was such an important step. It's important because it's one of Jesus' commands, so it's a mark of one's commitment to Jesus."

Children who grow up in Churches like the Baptist Church learn that they should be baptised only when they are prepared to accept the Christian faith for themselves. Baptisms take place in the presence of the whole congregation so the children are very familiar with what happens. There's a big pool at the front, under the floor, under boards. When someone is baptised the boards are taken up and the pool is filled with water. The person is lowered right under the water. This is called 'total immersion'.

"The boys wore trousers and white shirts and the girls wore long white dresses. Beforehand you felt very nervous really because the church was full and a lot of people had come whom you'd invited along – friends and family. The first thing I can remember was being helped down into the baptistry. You had to walk over to where the minister was standing and kneel down. The water came up to about chest level. You are asked: 'Do you confess Jesus Christ as Saviour and Lord?' and you say 'I do'. Then the minister puts his hands on your back and neck and pushes you forward into the water and the whole of your head goes under.

When you come up out of the water you turn round to the whole church and say 'Jesus is Lord' and in our church all the congregation answer 'Hallelujah'. It's an incredible feeling when they do it. Then the minister puts his hands on your head and blesses you. Immediately afterwards you feel incredibly happy, quite elated. You're surrounded by people who are genuinely very happy for you. It's also a witness to friends and relatives who perhaps have no interest in the church. It starts quite a lot of conversations with friends as to why you did it and why you believe in Jesus and in God.

One of the things you worry about – I don't know if you should – is whether you are going to be dropped or whether you are going to be picked up in time! So you've all these things going through your mind as well as all the symbolism of your old life passing away, like Jesus' death, and then as you come up out of the water it's like rising to a new life in Jesus. It's very special because it's so symbolic."

1 Read about the symbolism of baptism in Colossians 2.12.

2 Write to an Anglican vicar and a Baptist minister and ask whether they would be willing for you to interview them about baptism. Find out what happens at their church at a baptism, and ask them what they think about Infant Baptism and Believers' Baptism. If you tape the interview you will have an accurate record of it, and you could copy out parts of it for your class display.

In warm climates baptisms may take place out of doors. The people being baptised here are members of a Baptist church in Zaire, Africa.

Being confirmed

In Churches which have Infant Baptism, there is an opportunity for young people to confirm – to make their own – the promises which their godparents made on their behalf when they were babies. In the Anglican and Roman Catholic Churches this happens at a service called Confirmation.

"I was confirmed with about ten friends. We went to classes beforehand on Thursdays. We talked about the Bible, God, had a prayer session, and talked about the service – what it meant. We discussed different points of view and had jokes. One week we could ask the curate questions. I asked him what shape he'd like the church to be. He said he'd have it round with carpet on the floor so you could lie down or whatever. He doesn't like kneeling to pray."

"I was confirmed last December when I was thirteen. I decided that I was ready to be a full member of the church and understand Christ more. I didn't have to wear anything special for the service. My grandparents and godparents came. The Bishop comes – he gave the sermon. He talked to us, and it seemed shorter than usual because I was really listening. I was nervous before the service but when I sat down I had a few breaths to control myself. When I actually knelt in front of the Bishop I got the butterflies and started wondering whether I had the card the right way up, and whether he'd say my name right, but it was fine."

Here is one of the prayers used in the Anglican confirmation service:

'Almighty and everliving God,
you have given your servants new birth
in baptism by water and the Spirit,
and have forgiven them all their sins.
Let your Holy Spirit rest upon them:
the Spirit of wisdom and understanding;
the Spirit of counsel and inward strength;
the Spirit of knowledge and true godliness;
and let their delight be in the fear of the Lord.'

(*Alternative Service Book*)

An Anglican confirmation service.

The Bishop lays his hands on the head of each person in turn and says, 'Confirm, O Lord, your servant, John, with your Holy Spirit', so although in one way people are 'confirming' their baptismal vows, even more important, they are being 'confirmed', strengthened, by God.

Find out how Churches such as Methodist and United Reformed mark a young person's entry into membership of their Church.

Feeling you belong

*"My earliest memories are of going to church every Sunday with my parents. When you first went into the church it was quite overpowering, with the smell of the **incense**, and the bells. My favourite service was Midnight **Mass** at Christmas. The church was always completely packed. I used to get very sleepy, though. It isn't easy to sing carols at one in the morning when you are little."*

*"When I was small I loved going to **evensong** with my parents. I didn't really listen to anything that was being said, it was just the atmosphere. The church seemed to me, at that age, to be very big. There were two candles on the altar, and especially in winter, when the main lights were put out during the sermon, I gazed at these two candles – distant points of light in the darkness. It was a powerful experience."*

The local church

Since New Testament times Baptism has been the way by which people join the Christian Church – the Body of Christ – but this is a difficult idea for small children to grasp. When they are little it is the local church that they are aware of belonging to. Some churches help children to feel that they belong by letting them take part, perhaps by greeting people as they arrive and giving out hymn books and prayer books, or taking up the collection. Sometimes the children act a play for the congregation, or sing a song they have learnt.

"We always went to the morning service. Everyone was very welcoming. I usually went to sleep in the sermon! On the Sundays when we had family services it was great fun. We had lots of action songs, quizzes and visual aids. And we could really join in and help. We took it in turns to take up the collection and read from the Bible, and we even helped take the prayers."

In the Orthodox Church children go to church with their families from when they are babies, but the service is the **Liturgy** – Holy Communion – and there is lots to see.

"We always went to the Greek church, mainly to the cathedral, but sometimes we would go to smaller parishes. There are many Greek churches in London. Church was a fascinating place. There was always plenty to look at, even if you couldn't understand all that was going on. There were icons everywhere, and candles, and the smell of incense."

An Orthodox church has an iconostasis – a screen with icons on it.

Icons

Icons are not ordinary religious pictures. The Orthodox call them 'windows into heaven'. They say that icons are a way of teaching about the Christian faith. The artist is not trying to show what the person looked like. The painting is symbolic. For example, in icons of the Virgin and child, the infant Christ in Mary's arms looks more like a small adult than a baby. This is a way of showing the real significance of Christ for Christians. Painting icons is a religious activity. While the artist is working he or she will pray to the saint whose image is being painted.

'You can do your own thing'

"In the Russian church we have benches around the edge of the church, and there are some chairs for elderly people. But most people stand. There's a certain amount of moving about that you can do. Not having pews you can do your own thing. During the Gospel everyone is still, and they also stand during the preparation for communion, and when they are being censed. Otherwise you can stand, or you can sit if you want, you can kneel or you can bow to the floor. You can walk around even. You can go and greet people you know. It's a very free atmosphere. And we make the sign of the cross quite often during the Liturgy. It's a very active form of worship! You put your thumb and first two fingers together, and touch your forehead, chest, right shoulder and left shoulder, and often you bow as well. I loved doing it when I was a child."

Singing in a choir

Some children join a church choir, and that helps them to feel that they are an important part of the Church.

"I've been singing in the choir for six years now. I enjoy it, but it's hard work at festival times. I'm not bothered about singing in front of everyone now, because they know me."

"I joined the choir at a church in Birmingham when I was nine. There was quite a large West Indian congregation there, and a lot of my fellow choristers were West Indian. The highlight for us was when there was a test match at the Edgbaston cricket ground. In those days there used to be a test match service and a lot of the cricket team would come; we choir boys all grabbed their autographs after the service!"

"My parents sing in the choir in the Russian cathedral, so my sister and I always used to sit up in the choir with them. I must have been five when I started singing, but nine or ten is a more usual age. Singing plays a very important part in the Orthodox Liturgy, so you pick up the music just by going to church. Choir practices are usually only for special things."

Holy Communion

"After I was confirmed I could take communion. I think that taking the bread and wine means that you're taking Jesus into yourself. It helps you to feel closer to Jesus."

"I had my first Holy Communion and Confirmation when I was eight. I wore a white dress and a white veil. I remember what seemed like a very long walk up the aisle towards the Bishop. As a preparation for my first communion I made a few trips to the church, for basic teaching – why we were having the bread, what would happen in the service. I have a picture of the Bishop and me. I've also got a certificate to show that I've actually been confirmed. It's very nice to have that to look back on."

In the Roman Catholic Church it used to be the custom for children to be confirmed at about eight or nine, and then to be able to receive Holy Communion. Nowadays it is more common to allow children to take communion before they are confirmed. Children are also admitted to communion before confirmation in some parts of the Anglican Church, for example in Canada and New Zealand, and in some churches in Britain.

The Orthodox Churches, however, don't need to discuss how old children should be before they can take communion. Chrismation (anointing with oil) follows immediately after Baptism, and then immediately after that the baby is given communion.

"It's perfectly normal for children to take communion with the adults. Because my whole experience was Orthodox I'd never seen anything else. It was the most natural thing. I always liked taking communion. You are made to feel that it is something very special."

Receiving communion in a Russian Orthodox church.

Holy Communion is the central act of worship for Christians. Here are some accounts of it in different Churches:

*"In the Orthodox Church all those who are going to take communion gather in the centre of the church, **venerating** the icon which is in the middle of the church, and we stand with our hands folded on our shoulders. I was always told that you put your right hand underneath your left one, because when you go up to communion you don't cross yourself, and if your left hand is over your right it's more difficult, so you remember not to! The chalice is brought out and usually people prostrate themselves. Some people just bow, but children usually go right down. You first kneel, then put your hands down, then your head touches the floor.*

*Communion is given out of a big **chalice**, usually golden, and the bread is in the wine, which is warm because hot water has been put in it. You're given this in a spoon, and as the priest gives it to you he says your name. The priests have a remarkable memory for people. If they don't know your name they will ask. When you've received the body and blood of Christ, you're given some unconsecrated bread and wine."*

*"Something that's different in the Baptist Church is the communion. The minister blesses it all on the table, then the **deacons** bring the bread round to the congregation and you pass the plate from one to the other and eat the bread straight away to show that your faith is personal to you and your relationship with God is a personal one. When it comes to the wine you all have individual glasses but keep it until everyone has one, and drink it together to show that you are the body of Christ and to share in fellowship and communion together. The wine is non-alcoholic."*

"I was six when I had my first communion. It was a period of my life when I felt very religious, and wanting to be close to Jesus. I enjoyed going to communion very much. In those days in the Catholic Church you had to fast all night before having communion, so we went early in the morning, and then went back and had a quick breakfast before going to school."

Interview Christians who belong to as many different Churches as you can, and ask them to tell you how communion is celebrated in their Church. If they use a special prayer book, look up the order of the service. Then make a chart which shows what the service is called in each Church, what is said and done in the part of the service when members of the congregation receive communion, and how children are involved.

Communion in a Methodist church.

Fasting

"In the Orthodox Church you don't have to take communion every Sunday – it's up to the individual. You're supposed to fast as a preparation. How you fast depends on the family.

Sometimes people just don't eat before they go to church, but if you're quite strict about it you'd fast from the day before. That doesn't mean you won't eat anything. It just means you won't eat meat, or perhaps meat and dairy products. Fasting is something that is quite important in the faith. In our family we've not eaten meat on a Friday ever. We usually eat bean dishes and things like that. But with children it's a bit different. People are a bit more lenient."

Fasting is practised in many religions. In other books in this series you can learn about fasting in Islam and Judaism and Hinduism. From these and other resources find out about the place of fasting in each religion. Make a display which shows the place of fasting in each of the religions: who fasts, when they fast, what is given up, the reasons given for fasting, and what fasting means to those who practise it. (⟶ page 41 for fasting in Lent)

Confession

Repentance, saying that one is sorry for the wrong things that one has done, is an important part of Christian worship. Many children who are growing up in Christian families are encouraged to look back over the day that has just finished, and include the things they are sorry for in their bedtime prayers. And when they go to services in church they hear prayers of confession.

The Orthodox, Roman Catholics and some Anglicans also make an individual confession of their sins to God in the presence of a priest. In the Roman Catholic Church confession in now called the Sacrament of Reconciliation.

"In the Russian Church confession is closely tied to communion. You must go to confession before you go to communion. You don't go to communion every week; you go to church but you don't take communion. But a child will go to communion without going to confession for quite a number of years. The first time a child will go to confession depends very much on the child. Usually it's about eight, but some children are about ten or eleven without going to confession."

"The first time I went to confession, I was about eight or nine, after having my first communion. You're waiting in the church, and there's this big box, and people come out with a smile on their face – it's a relief having been in there – and you think, this enclosed box, and God's in there. To a child, he's actually in there, and you think that God is going to tap you on the shoulder and say, 'It's OK'!

I find that non-Catholics seem to think some very strange things about confession, that you go and pour out your sins and then it doesn't matter what you do. But it's not at all like that. Everybody does make mistakes in their life, and as long as you are truly sorry for them God will take those sins away, but that's only if you are truly sorry."

In a confessional box in a Roman Catholic church. The priest sits on the other side of the grille.

Taking part with the adults

Churches aren't just places where people go to worship on Sundays. They are communities of people, and there are many activities for members of churches to be involved in. Some of the activities are very enjoyable, and they help children to feel that the church is rather like a large family.

"We have a parish Pancake Party on Shrove Tuesday, and we have a Harvest Supper. People sing and act and have fun after the meal. One man always takes off the vicar. He's very good at it!"

"We went away on a parish weekend. The children had games and discussion while the adults met in their groups. It was really fun. We worked out a play and acted it for the congregation in the Sunday service."

Children really feel that they belong to the church when they are allowed to take part in the grown-ups' activities.

"I was fourteen when I was baptised, and the next week I was admitted as a member of the Baptist Church. Being a church member means you can go to church meetings and help make decisions about things, be part of a Bible study group. You are able to share together with other Christians and learn more together."

With other Churches

In many places Christians from different Churches meet together in someone's home for discussion groups or Bible study, perhaps during Lent. The children of Christian families will know that their parents are sharing with Christians from other **denominations**, but the children are more likely to be involved with members of other Churches when they are working to raise money for charities, or when there are combined activities at special times.

"In the past couple of years we've joined with the Anglicans for a service on Good Friday, and we join with the other churches several times a year now, at Christmas, at Whitsun and for the Harvest festival."

"On Palm Sunday there were processions from several local churches to the Old Pond, where we all met for a service. One of the curates came on a donkey."

People from different churches take part in a Good Friday procession on Hampstead Heath in London.

Through activities like these children come to learn that although there are different denominations, they all share the same faith and all belong to the religion called Christianity.

> 1 Make a list of the Christian denominations in your area. On an outline map of the area mark in where the different denominations meet for worship.
>
> 2 Find out what activities the churches in your area join together for.

Belonging to a worldwide Church

"I saw the Pope when he came to Baginton airport, just outside Coventry. We had to camp out overnight, which was fun. That was so that we could be near the front, as there were thousands and thousands of people. We had a service in the morning. It was boiling hot. I lay under the deckchair to get some shade. The Pope came round in his Popemobile, and he was only about a metre away. It was absolutely fantastic to have him so close."

Receiving communion from Pope John Paul at Coventry airport.

Roman Catholic children learn very early that they belong to a worldwide Church. They see the Pope on television, and they see film of him visiting many different countries. If the Pope comes to their country their families will try to take them to see him, even if for some of them it means making very long journeys.

Children who belong to one of the Orthodox Churches also learn very early about the Church in other lands. In a Greek Orthodox Church they will hear the Liturgy in the Greek language, and they may see priests who have come from Greece. They will discover that the ways in which they celebrate the festivals are similar to the ways in which they are celebrated in Greece.

"I've been to Greece many times. We were taken as a whole family three times when I was younger. After that I've just been by myself and stayed with friends and relatives."

In 1988 the Russian Church celebrated its **millennium** – a thousand years of Christianity in Russia – and this was marked in all the countries in which Russian Orthodox people live.

"There was a millennium concert in London with the Russian cathedral choir singing. And then we were invited to sing in various Anglican churches. We went to Birimingham, to the cathedral, to Winchester Cathedral, and we sang in Oxford.

But the highlight was singing at the Lambeth Conference. We celebrated **Vespers** *in Canterbury Cathedral, and for us they took all the chairs out of the cathedral – the great cathedral! There were all the bishops of the Anglican Communion, and there were representatives of other Churches. The Archbishop of Smolensk, from Russia was there, representing the Moscow* **Patriarchate***, and he spoke. It was a most tremendous experience."*

East and West

Early in its history Christianity was divided between the Eastern Church and the Western Church. The Orthodox Churches are part of the Eastern Church. There are a number of them, including the Armenian and the Serbian Churches. The main ones, however, are the Greek and Russian Churches. The head of each Orthodox Church is called a Patriarch.

"I went to Russia on a trip organised in connection with the millennium of the Russian Church. I was visiting the mother Church. You forgot what country you were in; you forgot the outside way of life. The Church was 'home'."

You don't have to be Greek or Russian, however, to belong to the Greek or Russian Church. Many people from other countries are attracted to the Orthodox form of worship, and they may decide to join an Orthodox Church.

"In the Russian Cathedral in London the choir sings in both Russian and English, though not all the choir members speak Russian. Russian was my first language – before English. It was spoken at home. But out of about forty people in the choir, fewer than ten are Russians. We have Greeks, Romanians, a Finnish woman, a Dutch woman, an American woman."

Find out from the churches in your area what links they have with the Church in other countries. You could start with the notice board and the bookstall in each church, but you would then need to ask the priest or minister whether there are any other links, or whether perhaps any of the members of the congregation have lived in other countries.

Belonging to a world religion

Christianity has spread to many countries across the world, just as other religions have done. Countries have their own cultures and their own kinds of society, so different customs and ways of doing things often become part of Christian practice.

*"Children go to weddings a lot more in Mexico than here. The boys are usually **acolytes**. They wear red tunics and they come in, in front of the bride, carrying candles, and at the end of the service they process out in front of the bride and bridegroom. They feel very important! They are usually between about three and eight or nine. At eight they start feeling they're a bit too old to be acolytes. The girls dress as little bridesmaids, in white, and they take care of the bride – or they think they do! They hold candles, and come in behind the bride. One or two of them are supposed to look after the bride's train, and see that she looks all right. My sister was one of the first in our family to get married, so there weren't many children around, but there were something like twenty-five or thirty children taking part. Friends' children are invited as well as relatives."*

"In the traditional religion in my part of Africa, the way to make sure that the community is looked after, that no one is too poor, is for a group of women, in turns, to go round the village, helping either ploughing the fields or growing maize, or doing some community work. This was always done on a Tuesday – I don't know why. They go as a group. And when some of these people became Christians they just carried over this practice."

In this Roman Catholic Mass everyone is sitting on the floor, which is the custom in Hindu **puja**, and the priest is wearing the saffron coloured robes of an Indian holy man. An Indian lamp stands in front of the low altar, and on the altar there are flowers, which are always associated with worship in India.

Sometimes, though, missionaries from the West, from countries such as Britain and America, thought that people who became Christians should give up their own culture. They thought that their converts might be tempted to return to their old religion if they continued to practise their traditional customs and rituals. This meant that children often felt torn between two different cultures.

"My grandfather was a convert of the very first missionaries in this part of Africa. In those days you were cut off from your culture and your tradition, so he left his village and went to the mission centre, and my parents were born there.

I was confirmed when I was thirteen. We were asked to choose a new name. I thought this would be a very good opportunity to choose an African name, and several of the others did too. I wanted to be called Tendai, which means 'thanksgiving' in Shona, but to my shock we were told we couldn't use these names because they were not the names of saints. So I was called Geraldine. It's changing now though; it's getting more African.

We haven't any children yet, but we do talk quite a lot about how we will bring them up. The main thing that I would do differently from the way I was brought up would be emphasising our African identity. We also talk about language. My husband comes from Mozambique, so he has a different mother tongue. He's learning mine, Shona, because we are going back to live in Zimbabwe. We do have English in common. It would be good to have a child with two languages, Shona and English."

Pilgrimage

Many Christians like to visit places that have a special meaning for the Christian faith. There are pilgrimage places in Britain, such as Walsingham in Norfolk, and Glastonbury in Somerset, Iona in Scotland, and Canterbury. In some parts of the country young people have their own pilgrimage.

"I've been to St Albans twice now at Easter. Most of the members of our youth group go. We walk from our village, and we carry a large wooden cross as a kind of witness to the people we pass on the way. Groups come from towns and villages all over the diocese. When we get to St Albans we have a great Easter festival service in the Abbey. It's an amazing feeling, and it helps you to realise what Easter is about."

Europe

"I'd love to go to Rome. And to see the Vatican. That's the one place I'd love to go to. If I ever get the money I'll go."

"I haven't made a pilgrimage yet. Lourdes would be a wonderful place to go to. My auntie has been. She brought my mum back some holy water. My auntie had had an operation on the cartileges of her knees. Being there helps the healing process."

There are Christian pilgrimage centres in many countries, especially in Europe. Some of these are St Peter's Church in Rome, Taizé and Lourdes in France, Fatima in Portugal and St James Compostella in Spain. About three million people visit Lourdes every year, and about two million visit Fatima.

Young people from many countries make a pilgrimage to Taizé in France. In this photo they are joining with the members of the Taizé Community for Saturday evening prayers.

Orthodox centres

Many of the pilgrimage centres in Europe are specially important to Roman Catholics, but in Greece and Russia the pilgrimage centres are more important to members of the Orthodox Churches. One of these is Kiev, the first city in Russia to which Christianity was taken.

"In Kiev we were taken to see the caves monastery. It's one of the oldest monasteries in Russia. It was built about the eleventh or twelfth century, and it's one of the centres of Orthodoxy. We were taken down by one of the monks into a cave. You go down with a lighted candle; it's the only lighting. The caves are really tunnels. They are white and they are quite small. You could almost touch the sides with your arms outstretched, and you can certainly reach the ceiling.

You also have the coffins of the monks. On either side there are little openings. Some of the monks used to wall themselves up there, and lead a totally solitary life, praying, underground in the darkness, and once a day one of the brothers would bring them food. It's quite strange going down a small tunnel, having all these bodies – saints. There are 110 saints in the two caves. It was so fascinating that I don't think anyone looked at their watches going in or coming out."

The Holy Land

The pilgrimage place that is important to all Christians is the land where Christianity first began. Christians call it the Holy Land. Many church organisations arrange tours for their members. These are very popular at Christmas and Easter.

"My teacher went to Israel last year. She showed us slides of the places she had been to. We saw pictures of Jerusalem, and the Church of the Nativity in Bethlehem where Jesus was born, and Nazareth, and the Sea of Galilee where he called his disciples. She says she wants to go back to Jerusalem at Eastertime so that she can take part in the procession on Good Friday that follows the way that Jesus went to the cross."

> Choose a Christian pilgrimage centre and find out as much as you can about it. Prepare a guide booklet which would help people to understand why it is such an important place to Christians.

Opposite: A Good Friday procession in Jerusalem follows Jesus' way to the cross.

Times and seasons

Celebrating Christmas

"In Germany we celebrate Christmas on 24 December. You prepare for Christmas and go to church in the morning.

The Christmas tree goes up on Christmas Eve. It's decorated with tiny wooden toys made for children. You have real candles, and underneath the tree are the presents, and a crib. The room it's in is locked. A bell rings and you can go into the room. All the candles are lit. You stand there gazing. We gather round the tree and pray or sing. It is all very exciting, and something very deep inside."

No one knows the date of Jesus' birthday, but in the fourth century the Church decided to celebrate it on 25 December – the Roman festival of the Unconquered Sun – and gradually customs from other mid-winter festivals were adopted and given new meanings.

Christmas is a popular Christian festival, but the way it is celebrated varies.

"Christmas in Africa was lovely. When we were in Rwanda everyone went to church on Christmas Day. The crowds were so great that we held the service outside. They tend not to give each other presents. If they can, they make some special clothes for the coming year, and wear them on Christmas Day to honour Jesus. They like to make a gift to the church – perhaps money or something they have, like a sheep from their flock or some special food they have grown."

"Christmas for us in the Russian Church is 7 January. We have our main service on the 6th at 6.30pm – the Eve – because we have the Jewish tradition of the day starting at sundown. I always thought it was very good to have a later Christmas, because I think that Christmas in Britain tends to be all to do with presents and eating and watching television."

Epiphany

"Epiphany, 6 January, is a public holiday in Germany. In our village children dress up as the kings, and go from house to house. The moment someone opens the door we start singing. People give us money, cookies, apples, oranges or whatever. It's arranged by the church, and everything we get is distributed to people in need."

'Epiphany' means 'showing'. The Western Churches celebrate the showing of the Christ child to the **Magi** at Epiphany – a symbol for Christians of the significance of Jesus for the whole world. The Orthodox Churches still follow an ancient tradition of celebrating Jesus' baptism at Epiphany; they celebrate the showing of the Christ child to the Magi as well as to the shepherds on Christmas day.

An Indian artist puts the visit of the wise men to Jesus into an Indian setting.

1 Interview as many people as possible to find out what Christmas traditions they have in their family.

2 Make a survey of the different church services and other activities which help Christian children to understand the meaning of Christmas.

Celebrating Easter

"In Germany you get up early on Easter Day. Your parents hide eggs and chocolates and you hunt for them. You take a lamb made out of dough, eggs and a ham to Mass. They are blessed and then you go home to breakfast. It's the best tasting ham and eggs you have all year long. It's a very joyful day."

Each year, as Easter draws near, shops are full of Easter eggs. The name 'Easter' comes from a pre-Christian goddess – Oestre – who symbolised the coming of new life in spring. Christians took over the custom of giving eggs, and gave it a new meaning. Eggs symbolise for Christians the new life that Jesus brings them.

Decorated eggs

"Children at school didn't know what to make of it if I brought coloured eggs in my packed lunch. In the Orthodox Church we have a tradition of dyeing eggs. We draw the cross, and write the initials of 'Christ is risen!' in Russian on the eggs. We just use a felt-tipped pen. There are many red eggs, but we also do other colours – blue, purple, yellow, green, orange. It's the children's job to paint the eggs."

Painted eggs.

Decorated eggs play a very important part in the Easter celebrations of the Orthodox Church. Some people paint elaborate patterns on their eggs, other people dye them. Here a member of the Greek Orthodox Church describes the custom in her family.

"We make our own red eggs on the Saturday. We normally make enough to last for a couple of weeks. You boil them long and hard with a red dye which is a powder. You add vinegar to the hot water – that makes them take the dye. Then you polish them with olive oil.

We have a special breakfast with red eggs. As you take your egg from the bowl you smash it with someone else's egg. The one who smashes it on top says **'Christos anesti'***. We have competitions to see whose is the master egg. Sometimes you may not get to eat your egg because it won't break. Sometimes you find it lasts a week and you're still the champion."*

Try making your own decorated eggs for a class display.

Food is an important part of celebrations in all religions, and special foods are associated with the season of Easter. Popular Easter foods in the Western Churches are hot cross buns and simnel cake.

Easter feast

"The feast the Greeks have on Saturday night usually includes a chicken soup – Avgolemona, which means egg and lemon. We have that on Easter night, but not till after the midnight service. We have all my cousins over, and we sometimes have friends as well. It's quite a big feast! The meal goes on for a couple of hours. There's wine, and there are red eggs on the table, and there are flowers all over the house.

We also make a Greek cake called tsoureki, which is a yeast bread. It's got currants in it, and it's got a spice which is special to this bread. You make it in plaits. We make them shiny by painting raw egg on top. I think these foods are traditional; certainly in our family it's always been the case. We do have them at other times of the year, but we always make them at Easter."

Symbolism of light

The Orthodox Church has a service at midnight on Easter Eve. Roman Catholic Churches and many Anglican churches also have an 'Easter Vigil' on the Saturday evening. The service is full of the symbolism of light and darkness.

The paschal candle is lit from the Easter fire in this Anglican Easter vigil service.

"The service in the Russian cathedral in London starts in the middle of the night, about twenty to twelve. Everyone gathers. There's no light in the church – that represents the tomb, and the shroud of Christ is lying in front of the sanctuary. It's painted as an icon. The shroud is taken into the sanctuary, and everything is dark and still. The men of the choir have gone into the sanctuary, and when it's twelve they start singing, very quietly at first: 'We praise thy holy resurrection; thy angels sing in heaven, and let us praise thee with a pure heart.' That's a very rough translation; we always sing it in Russian. They just keep singing it, then the women start singing it as well. It's very joyful.

Everyone has candles. We light them from the little oil lamps that burn in front of the icons. The procession round the outside of the cathedral starts when the main candle is brought out of the sanctuary, followed by men and boys carrying icons. You stop at the closed doors. The priest sings three times, 'Christ is risen from the dead', and the third time the choir joins in. Then the doors of the church open, and you enter into light. The priest goes from the west door to the sanctuary, crying 'Christ is risen!', and everyone answers 'He is risen indeed'. This greeting is done in three languages in our church – Russian, Greek and English.

Then we have the Liturgy. It goes on till about 3.30. Children are often put to bed on the floor during the Liturgy, and then woken up for communion, but some stay up for all of it.''

''At school it was rather strange when our Russian Orthodox Easter fell in term time. We were lucky because we were allowed to be off school for the Friday, and sometimes the Thursday as well. Children at school thought it was very weird. You're out of step with people, but you're in step with something that's very important to you and your family.''

Holy Week

''You can't really understand Easter without having Holy Week. You have a very vivid account of Jesus' **passion**, *you're virtually re-living it in the church.''*

During Holy Week Christians remember the events in the last week of Jesus' life. Many churches hold daily services, and music and drama are often used to re-tell the story of Jesus' passion.

''One year we had a real donkey leading the procession in our church. We all processed around the church behind the donkey, singing and waving our palm crosses.''

**Maundy
Thursday**

In many churches the candles are removed on Maundy Thursday, and the altar cross is removed or covered. In some churches a vigil of prayer is kept throughout the night.

"The Maundy Thursday service in our church is a very solemn one, with time for silent prayer. The bareness and the silence remind us of the way in which Jesus faced his death alone. His followers slept while he prayed and then they deserted him."

Find out about the Royal Maundy ceremony in Britain, and show how it is related to the events of Holy Week.

There are many different ways in which Christian children experience the celebration of Jesus' death and resurrection.

Here a Greek Orthodox girl describes some of the Easter traditions in her family:

Good Friday

"We always go to the Greek Church on Good Friday. There's a procession. They carry his **epitaphius** *round the church – it's a sort of replica of the entombment, a cloth with the body of Christ painted on it. They put it on a stand so that it can be held. They carry it round the church and you go under it. That symbolises going into the tomb with Christ. There are flowers everywhere – a lot of red. Red is a festive colour, and it's the biggest celebration of the year.*

Good Friday is a strict fast. You don't eat even olive oil. No dairy products whatsoever, and no fish and no meat. On Good Friday the Greeks eat lentils.

Easter Eve

On the Saturday we always take our communion early, about 8 o'clock. And straight after we have a tradition of going to a really nice baker's around the corner, and we buy croissants. That's how we celebrate having had communion, but we still don't eat meat for the rest of the day, or dairy products. (For the Easter feast → *page 33.)*

We go to church about half past ten in the evening. At midnight they turn all the lights out, and they have one candle lit in the sanctuary – the **Paschal** *candle – and from that light everyone else takes a light. That's when they start saying 'Christ is risen!'.*

Children love the candles. It's a very impressive experience. With our Paschal candle the great thing for children was to try to get it home if you

Kissing the icon of Christ in a Greek Orthodox church.

weren't staying for the Liturgy. Sometimes it would be raining. Once, I remember, it was snowing. I remember driving home in the car with these candles. We managed a couple of times to get it home. It's a great feeling. You can then light new candles at home from your Paschal light. It just makes it special.''

1 Interview Christians from different Churches and make a display to show how their traditions help their children to understand the meaning of Easter.

2 Find out what customs are traditionally associated with Easter Monday, and how they are linked with the meaning of Easter.

Round the Christian year

"Some of the special times in our family are when there are festivals."

The main beliefs of a religion are expressed through the important times and seasons which make up the cycle of the religious year. Children become aware of these beliefs through the ways in which the festivals are celebrated and through the stories which are re-told at each festival.

Calendar

The calendar which was in use in the Roman empire when Christianity began is called the Julian calendar, because it was devised by Julius Caesar. It was discovered that this calendar did not correspond exactly to the time the earth took to go round the sun, so in the sixteenth century Pope Gregory XIII revised it. This Gregorian calendar is the one which has been adopted for general international use.

The Russian Orthodox Church still uses the Julian calendar. This is why its festivals fall on different dates ⟶ page 30.

Date of Easter
The date of Easter can fall anywhere between 21 March and 25 April. Christians celebrated the resurrection of Jesus on the Sunday after the Jewish Passover so its date came to be fixed by the Paschal full moon. 'Paschal' comes from the Hebrew for Passover. This is why the name for Easter in many languages is derived from the Hebrew word '**pesach**', e.g. 'Pâques' in French. (The dates for Easter right up to the year 2025 can be found in the *Alternative Service Book*.)

Opposite is a chart of the seasons of the Christian year and its main festivals and fasts.

The liturgical colour which will be used in the Anglican and Roman Catholic Churches for such things as the altar frontal and vestments are shown in brackets on the chart.

One of the New Testament readings included in the *Alternative Service Book* **lectionary** for use in Anglican churches is shown for each festival or fast day.

Seasons of the Christian year

Season	Special Days	New Testament Reading
Advent (*violet*)	Advent Sunday	Luke 21: 25–33
Christmas (*white or gold*)	Christmas Day	Luke 2: 1–20
Epiphany (*white or gold*)	Epiphany	Matthew 2: 1–12
Lent (*violet*)	Ash Wednesday	Matthew 6: 16–21
Holy Week	Palm Sunday (*red*) Maundy Thursday (*red or violet; white at Holy Communion*) Good Friday (*red*) Holy Saturday/Easter Eve (*white or gold at Holy Communion*)	Matthew 21: 1–13 John 13: 1–15 John 19: 1–37 Matthew 27: 57–66
Easter	Easter Day (*white or gold*) Ascension Day (*white*)	John 20: 1–18 Acts 1: 1–11
Pentecost	Pentecost/Whitsunday (*red*) Trinity Sunday (*white or gold*)	Acts 2: 1–11 John 14: 8–17

Advent

The season of Advent begins four Sundays before Christmas. 'Advent' means 'coming'. It is the time when Christians prepare themselves both to celebrate Jesus' coming at Christmas and his coming at the end of time. The Orthodox Church has a forty day fast leading up to Christmas.

ADVENT SUNDAY Luke 21:25–33

"We have an Advent wreath in our church. It's made of evergreens with four candles set in it. We light one on each Sunday in Advent. At home we have an Advent calendar, and you're allowed to open one door each day. In some calendars the doors have chocolates behind them."

Christmas

CHRISTMAS DAY Luke 2:1–20

Epiphany

"In Germany we have a carnival between Epiphany and Lent. We really celebrate before we go into Lent! We have a procession on Shrove Tuesday. Nobody works. People dress up and decorate big carts and wagons. In the processions you throw confetti."

Shrove Tuesday: 'Shrove' comes from 'to shrive', which means 'to be forgiven'. People used to go to church on this day to confess their sins and so be ready for Lent.

A carnival before lent begins in Rio de Janiero, Brazil.

Lent

Lent is the season of preparation for Easter. Originally it was the time when people fasted and received teaching as a preparation for their baptism on Holy Saturday. It later became a time for all Christians to fast and prepare for Easter. When Lent was kept really strictly people didn't eat meat, animal fats, dairy products or sweet things, and they had only one meal a day – in the evening.

Many hymns which Christians sing in Lent refer to Jesus' temptations in the wilderness before he began his ministry.

"In our church we have a Lent project each year. We learn about people in another country and raise money for something special they need."

Find out the ways in which Christians in your area keep Lent. Use words and pictures to show what they do and how it helps them to prepare for Easter.

ASH WEDNESDAY Matthew 6:16–21

"On Ash Wednesday we take our palm crosses from the previous year and have them burnt in a bowl at the front of the church, actually in the service. Then the ashes are placed on our foreheads in the sign of the cross during communion. It shows that you are sorry for all the wrong things that you have done."

Ash Wednesday is the first day of Lent. It falls in the seventh week before Easter. Its name comes from the ashes which are used in Anglican and Roman Catholic churches.

Holy Week

PALM SUNDAY Matthew 21:1–13

MAUNDY THURSDAY John 13:1–15

GOOD FRIDAY John 19:1–37

HOLY SATURDAY/EASTER EVE Matthew 27:57–66

Easter

EASTER DAY John 20:1–18

> Find out when Easter falls this year. Make a list of the days which are linked to the date of Easter – from Ash Wednesday to Easter Day. Add this year's dates, and the appropriate liturgical colours.
>
> Then read the New Testament passages and make a display to show how these passages remind Christians of events in the life of Jesus.

ASCENSION DAY Acts 1:1–11

"In Germany we have a holiday on Ascension Day. In our village the Catholics have a procession. We walk to four altars which have been decorated with flowers and set up in different parts of the village – north, south, east and west. This is a way of showing that the whole world belongs to Jesus."

Ascension Day falls on a Thursday, forty days after Easter (⟶ Acts 1:3). Many Ascension Day hymns express the Christian belief that the ascension of Jesus symbolised his kingship.

Pentecost

PENTECOST/WHITSUNDAY Acts 2:1–11

Pentecost falls seven weeks after Easter Day. It celebrates the beginning of the Christian Church, and so used to be a special day for baptisms. The custom of wearing white for baptism led to its being called 'White Sunday' or 'Whitsun'.

"At Whitsun the Christians from all the churches have a procession through the town. We carry banners for each church."

TRINITY SUNDAY John 14:8–17

Trinity Sunday is the Sunday after Pentecost. It celebrates Christians' belief in God as Father, Son and Holy Spirit.

In the Anglican Church the season of Trinity Sunday up to Advent used to be called Trinity, and its liturgical colour was green, symbolising growth in the Christian faith. The name has been changed to Pentecost, and it now refers to the period from Pentecost to the Ninth Sunday before Christmas. In the Roman Catholic Church the Sundays between Pentecost and Advent are called 'Ordinary Sundays of the year'.

An altar frontal for Pentecost made by children.

The Christian calendar also includes a number of saints' days. Choose one of these, perhaps the patronal festival of a local church. Find out what it was about this person's life which made the Christian Church describe him or her as a saint.

Learning about the faith

Learning at home

"As a child I just accepted Christianity as a fact of life. My parents didn't talk about it an awful lot when we were small; but they lived it. It was just there. We weren't expected to spend a lot of time studying the Bible or anything like that, but Christianity was always there in the background of the home. It was a part of day to day life."

"Mum and Dad are very thoughtful, and conscious of being Christians and having a Christian attitude about things. So when they're tempted to have a moan about somebody they say, 'We should give them the benefit of the doubt. They may have something getting on their nerves.' It's not that they are amazing halo people. It just changes the way they think."

The most important influence on children who are growing up in Christianity is their family. Children see what their parents do, how they treat people, and how they react to the sad things that happen as well as to the happy things. They see that the Christian faith is very important to their parents, and as they grow up they gradually learn what it means for themselves.

"When we were very young we had to go to church once on a Sunday, but as we grew older my parents respected our individuality and let us make up our own minds. My parents always try to guide us in the right direction but not force us. They say it is our decision, we have to make up our minds for ourselves."

Prayers

Worship is a very important part of being a Christian. Children learn about public worship when they go to church, but they learn about personal prayer in their family.

"My mother taught me to pray. From when I was one or two she prayed beside me at bedtime, and I gradually learnt the prayers – the Our Father and the Hail Mary, and a little prayer which was to the Virgin and a guardian angel, to protect me. I enjoyed saying the prayers very much, and praying for my parents and grandparents and friends and cousins. It became part of my life to say prayers at night."

Many evangelical Christians set aside a time every day for the whole family to be together in worship. Prayers will be **extempore**, not taken from a book, and the children will be encouraged to pray aloud, to thank God for the good things that have happened to them, to tell him that they are sorry for the wrong things they have done, and to ask him to help them in whatever they will be doing during the day.

"We've tried to have family prayers and a reading from the Bible at breakfast time as well as at bedtime because having a prayer time in the morning puts God central in our lives."

When children are little they want to do what their parents are doing, like this small girl:

"Daddy wakes up very early and goes downstairs. He gets the Bible from his study and goes into the kitchen, finds the page and starts praying to God. I come rushing down and we have a little quiet time together 'cos we say lots of prayers to God and read passages from the Bible."

45

Doing

The words which are used in religion are often difficult for children to understand but they enjoy doing actions.

"When we were little we used to take it in turns to say grace before the meal, but now we have a 'Quaker' grace: we all join hands round the table and have a few moments' silence. I like that, it gives us a nice feeling of togetherness."

There are many things for the children of Roman Catholic or Orthodox families to do, such as lighting candles, using a **rosary** in prayer, or making the sign of the cross.

"I remember when I was first taken to church, you had to kneel and make the sign of the cross. That was probably my first time of doing the sign of the cross. My mother got me into the routine of doing it when we were praying at home. It's quite nice to have this individual sign which you do."

Seeing

Children also learn from what they see. Evangelical Christian families may have pictures like Holman Hunt's famous *The Light of the World*, or perhaps a framed text from the Bible. Roman Catholic families may have a **crucifix** or an image of the Madonna and child. Orthodox families usually have an icon in every room of the house, and the children will have an icon of their own patron saint in their bedroom.

An Orthodox person's patron saint is the one whose name he or she has been given at Baptism, and the saint's festival will be kept as the person's 'Name Day'. For many people it is an even more important day than their birthday.

An Orthodox family turns towards the icons to pray before their meal.

Make a survey of children and young people who belong to different Churches to discover what actions they learn to do, and what they have in their homes which help them to express what is important in their religion.

Learning with others

"One of my earliest memories of icons was when I went to Sunday School, and we were talking about Christmas, which we call the Nativity. Father Michael took us into the church and showed us the icon of the Nativity on the iconostasis. There is the cave, the donkey and the cow, and Mary lying there, and Jesus being bathed, and you have this blue semi-circle above, and a blue line coming down and a star which is pointing to Jesus. You even have the three kings there, bringing gifts, although in the story that happened later. It's a way of seeing what the feast is about. The icon was familiar, but once you know the story you know what to look out for in the icon."

In countries where there are large communities of Orthodox Christians it is not usual to have Sunday Schools; the children learn with their families and in the Liturgy at church, but in countries like Britain some churches have organised classes to help the children learn more about the faith.

The Roman Catholic Church has always encouraged its members to send their children to Roman Catholic schools, where learning about the faith is part of the school curriculum, but in recent times more emphasis has been put on the children learning from their parents. Some churches have special schemes to help parents to talk with their children about what it means to be a member of the Christian faith.

Most Protestant churches have a Sunday School or Children's Church which meets on a Sunday morning. In some churches the children spend part of the time with the adult congregation and part of the time in their classes, perhaps with their own act of worship. In many Anglican churches the children join the adult congregation in time to go up to the altar rail with their parents; they receive a blessing from the priest if they are not old enough to be allowed to be given the communion bread and wine.

"Now I'm eleven I've left Sunday School. I'm really sad to have left. We started with a prayer and sang, then split into groups. At half-term we made altar frontals for Easter and Pentecost." (⟶ page 43)

"I went to Sunday School from the age of about three. Each week we were given a special stamp with a religious picture on it. The highlight at that age was sticking the stamp on a card – I can still taste the glue!"

An icon of the Nativity.

More grown up

Some Sunday Schools take children as young as three or four. By the time children are ten or eleven they may feel that they are too grown-up for Sunday School, so many churches have a different kind of organisation for the older ones.

"Pathfinders is for ten to fourteen years olds. There are about thirty in our group and we meet every Tuesday. We play games like indoor hockey, and then split into groups for discussion. You get to know everybody and can put all points of view and learn together. We bring God into it, and learn about being a Christian. We discuss passages from the Bible. And we go on outings like ice-skating. It helps in being a Christian.

Every Whitsun we go away for five days to a Christian youth centre. We can play football, tennis, and go swimming and go-karting. We do duties like washing-up in teams. We go on outings and have meetings in the morning and evening when we sing and have talks by a special leader. Each time there seems to be a favourite song. We sang it to everybody in church when we got back."

"Once we're about twelve the vicar lets us help with baptisms. We show the parents and godparents where to stand, and give them the Baptism cards and the candles to hold. It's good. It makes you feel you are part of the Church."

"Our youth programme starts at thirteen. We go to church for the first twenty minutes, and then we go off to the village hall for a film or discussion. Then we have coffee afterwards at a leader's house, and we meet mid-week for a games evening. Then we have a week away every year. Sometimes we learn basic things about Jesus, the Bible and being a Christian. Other times we talk about current topics and how being a Christian affects it. It's good to have people to talk to and help you, especially if you are the only Christian in your class at school."

At school

Young people from Christian families also have an opportunity to think about their own faith in religious studies at school.

"We're learning about festivals of light, and we're going to put our display up in the hall. I didn't know that light was so important in other religions. It's made me think about light in Christianity."

Part of a multi-faith topic on festivals in a London secondary school.

"In the junior school we learnt about the kinds of places religions have for worship, and we went on visits to a mosque and a synagogue and then to a church."

"As I grew older I had a lot of questions raised in my mind in current affairs and religious education – did God really exist, why is there so much suffering in the world, why does God allow it? I struggled with other questions too, like is Christianity the only way to God or do the other religions have an equally valid path to God. I really wanted to sort out the answers so I did a lot of research, reading, talking to people, reading the Bible, so I was able to understand more myself and be able to explain it to others. I questioned just about everything – whether God is real, whether he did create the world, what he's doing, why. As I questioned all these things I came to the conclusion that God is real, that he does love and care for us, and I came out really with my Christian faith much stronger than it had been before."

Meeting the Bible

"We always used to have a Bible story as well as another story at bedtime. My brother and I took it in turns to choose the Bible story. Our favourite Old Testament story was Esther. We waited in suspense to see if she'd be saved, and her people too. When we had stories about Jesus we used to imagine that we were in the crowd watching him. Paul's shipwreck was another favourite. Later we had notes to help us understand the Bible, with questions and puzzles to do."

Read the story of Paul's shipwreck on the island of Malta. It is in chapters 27 and 28 of the Acts of the Apostles.

A page from the Lindisfarne Gospels.

"I read the Bible at home and take it to Pathfinders. I know lots of the stories now – about Jesus' crucifixion, Jesus' birth, the parables, Adam and Eve, but I can't say chapter and verse. We've got the Good News Bible at home but we use the New English Bible at school."

The Christian Bible is not a 'book'; it is really a whole library of books, which were written down over a period of nearly a thousand years. Most of it is far too difficult for children to understand, so when they are little they have stories from parts of the Old and New Testaments. Children's Bibles are made up only of stories, though many children also own a copy of the whole Bible. They also hear the Bible read in Church and they know that their parents read it, so they learn that it is important to Christians even if they are still too young to read it.

"My favourite Bible was a present when I was a bridesmaid. It's white with silver edging and it's got a little red marker. Some words are easy to understand, some aren't."

"I've got two Bibles. One's a big Children's Bible with pictures in it. I read it by myself. I pretend it's a school and I read it to my little puppet cat, 'cos he hardly knows anything about God."

Not just stories

As children get older they discover that there are many different kinds of writing in the Bible.

"My favourite passage in the Bible is in Paul's letter to the Corinthians, about love. I come back to it time and time again, for it shows how you should treat other people. When I'm under pressure I remember about putting on the armour of God."

---

1 Find and read the passages this girl refers to in the New Testament: 1 Corinthians 13 and Ephesians 6:13–17.

2 Choose any Bible story. Read it in a Children's Bible and in different versions, e.g., the official Churches' translations, such as the New English Bible, and translations made by groups of Christians, such as the Good News Bible or the New International Version. Make a list of the differences you find, especially between the Children's Bible and ordinary Bibles.

Links with the past

"We were very fortunate that my father was so knowledgeable about history. When we went anywhere on our holidays we'd pop into churches, and he never seemed to need to pick up a guide book to find out what had happened in that place, what the history of it was. I think that gave you the sense of continuity of Christianity over the centuries. My father loved the tradition, the feeling that this had been going on for a very long time, and this came over to us as children.

When I was about ten my father was co-author of a book on the history of the English Bible. It was serialised on radio, on Children's Hour – ten episodes, every Sunday evening. It was very exciting. You learnt all about the Reformation, and Tyndale's Bible and all that sort of thing."

Find out about William Tyndale, who translated the New Testament into English in the sixteenth century. What is it about his story that might make a ten year old describe it as 'exciting'?

The Christian Church is nearly two thousand years old, and many things have happened to it in that time. In all sorts of ways children become aware of the past. Here are some of them: learning about the customs which gradually became associated with Christmas and Easter; hearing stories of the saints, such as Francis, or Christians who helped to change society, such as Lord Shaftesbury. And of course, when they have stories from the New Testament they are learning about the very beginning of Christianity.

Links with Judaism

"The Orthodox have a very strong sense of coming from Judaism. The word for Easter in Russian is **pascha***, from pesach, the Hebrew word for Passover. I was always aware of the links with Judaism. Maybe it's a strong sense of tradition, the continuity, with the early Church and Palestine. You can't divorce the two. If you look at the life of Jesus you have to see it in its Jewish setting. You can't understand the story of the Good Samaritan unless you know what Samaritan means.*

For the Orthodox the idea of continuity is so important. How can you understand the Church without the whole experience of the early Church, and the people who personally knew Jesus, and knew the disciples and their teaching? Then you have all those councils, trying to put clearly into words what we believe in. The Apostles had the Lord's Prayer, and they had the Jewish form of worship, but they didn't have the Creed, and they didn't have the New Testament."

In the early centuries of the Church's history there were meetings called Ecumenical Councils, when Christian leaders met to discuss how to express what Christians believed about God, Jesus, the Holy Spirit and the Church. These Councils produced the Apostles' Creed and the Nicene Creed.

Make a list of ways in which children might learn about the past of Christianity. Add your own ideas to those which are mentioned in this chapter. Think of a good way to present this information for your display.

Opposite: Members of a youth camp on the island of Iona learn about the history of Iona as they act scenes from the past.

Understanding beliefs

"When I was about four my mother taught me the Apostles' Creed. She taught me secretly as a surprise for my father. I obviously didn't understand it, but I felt thrilled when I recited it to him. It also meant that I could join in with it at church, once I could say it fast enough."

Small children like to be able to do what the grown-ups are doing. But many Christian beliefs are difficult for them to understand.

"I couldn't grasp the idea of Jesus being 'part' of God, because all the stories were about the first century – he was a man with a flowing head-dress, flowing robe and sandals. It made him seem like a distant figure of history. Of course in human form he was part of history."

In some symbols of the Trinity God the Father is represented by a hand, God the Holy Spirit by a dove, and God the Son by either the figure of Jesus or a cross.

'Who made God?'

"When I was little I kept asking my parents, 'Who made God?' I had been told that God made the world, but I was very puzzled about where God came from. I remember feeling really frustrated that they couldn't tell me."

Sometimes adults try to explain Christian beliefs – theology – to children in simple terms.

"I remember we had a little image of the Trinity. You know, the traditional bearded man, and Christ next to him, on the cross, and a little dove at the top, and I remember my mother telling me that that was God the Father and God the Son and God the Holy Spirit. At that age you just accept things; you start thinking about what they really mean later."

Christianity began as a movement within Judaism, so the first Christians used Jewish ways of thinking to express their beliefs, like talking of God as Father. Then, as the religion spread into other countries, Christians began to use Greek ways of thinking. One example of this is describing the Trinity as 'three persons in one': in those days an actor in the Greek theatre would wear a mask – a 'persona' – to show the audience what kind of character he was playing. The expression 'dramatis personae' – the 'characters of the drama' – is still used for the cast of a play today. Christian theologians certainly didn't want to say that God is just an actor; they were trying to find a way of saying that there is only one God, that they didn't worship three separate Gods – Father, Son and Holy Spirit.

"My favourite hymn when I was little was
'Immortal, invisible, God only wise
In light inaccessible hid from our eyes.
Most blessed, most glorious, the Ancient of Days,
Almighty, victorious, thy great name we praise.'
I liked it much better than the children's hymns we sang at Sunday School. I didn't know what the words meant, but they created a wonderful impression of God as someone great and very majestic."

There are many different ways in which Christian children learn about God and Jesus. Some of their ideas come from Bible stories, and some from what they hear adults say. When they take part in worship in church, what they see and do and the atmosphere in the church are as important as the actual words of the prayers and the sermon.

"I don't think you listen to sermons till you're about fifteen or sixteen, though in our church they're usually pretty short. I don't think we teach much about God in the Orthodox Church. He's just there, self-evident. Obviously if you follow the services you pick up something. If you're taught about icons, you learn about aspects of God and Jesus in that way."

Picturing God   Children try to imagine what God is like, and the picture they have in their minds is influenced by what they already know about the world.

"I thought of God as a man – very big. I imagined he had a beard. This was my picture of a loving African grandfather, with hair grown white, and a big beard. And he was sitting down, with a big lap to contain all his grandchildren – very welcoming. Sadly, he was not black. Jesus wasn't black either. Even now it's something I think about. It was like worshipping foreign gods. It may be changing now, but it takes a long time, because all the pictures and images we had were European – as if God was English! But of course Satan was black. The notion of black as bad and white as good was very sad for us. It meant that you were starting to doubt your own self, your identity."

All the figures are African in this Nigerian carving of Jesus standing before Pilate.

*"The teaching we had as children about life after death was the old traditional Catholic framework of heaven, hell and **purgatory**. I remember having problems trying to imagine what hell would be like, but then I never felt that I was in danger of going to hell. But everybody said that almost certainly you would go to purgatory, even if it was only for a short while, and purgatory was like a kind of hell – there was fire. I remember trying to get used to the idea of heat. I remember going into the shower, turning on the hot tap, and standing underneath it to see what it was like. I found that after a while it got quite bearable. I didn't know that it was running cooler because there wasn't much hot water left, so I thought that purgatory wouldn't be so bad after all!"*

Religions use imagery – picture language – for talking about God and other things such as life after death, which can't be known about by using the five senses. This can be puzzling for children, because they tend to take the picture language literally, and think that it is an actual description.

Purgatory is believed by some Christians to be where people who are not really wicked spend some time after death, until they have been punished for their bad deeds and are ready to 'go' to heaven – rather like having a good wash to get ready for a party.

Make a list of Christian beliefs that you find it difficult to understand, and invite a Christian minister to come and help you discuss them.

Growing in the faith

"My sister and I were lucky, growing up in a clergy household. Many of the visitors to the house would be clergy, so there was a lot of religious discussion. We couldn't understand most of it, but it helped us to feel part of a religious group, and very much members of the Christian faith."

A childlike faith

"When I was about three I heard a speaker at church talking about asking Jesus to be your friend. That evening when we were having bedtime prayers, I said to my mother that I would like Jesus to be my friend. Obviously I didn't understand the theology or anything about the Bible. All I understood at that stage was that I wanted Jesus to be my friend. As I grew bigger and gradually understood more I needed to let my faith catch up with the way I was growing up."

Many very young children growing up in Christian families have what is called a childlike faith. It often means a great deal to them, but they are too young to know all that is involved in being a Christian, so as they grow up their faith has to grow too.

A mature faith

"I was brought up in a Christian family but when I was about fourteen I rebelled and didn't want to be part of the church at all. Then, to my dismay, when I was about sixteen God spoke to me. I was just lying in bed and I started thinking about what I was doing with my life. It was almost as if God was saying, 'Why have you gone away from me?' I tried to go to sleep but this thought kept coming, 'You're not happy, you know the way you are behaving is wrong. Why don't you come back to me?' Then, very quietly, a feeling that God was there and all the things I'd been brought up with I knew to be true, and that Jesus was alive. So I just said out loud, 'Please Jesus come into my heart'. I felt very peaceful. The next day I went round to tell the leader of our youth group – this is what I've done and I'm going to need help. They were really glad too."

Some people can look back to an exact moment when they accepted the Christian faith, when a particular experience marked a turning-point in their lives. For other people, growing in the Christian faith is a much more gradual experience. They are aware of all sorts of influences through their life which have helped them to come to a mature faith.

Two servers assist the priest in an Anglican church.

"There was a time when I didn't think that making the sign of the cross during the Liturgy was particularly important – at the beginning of my teens – but then I started listening to the words. In a way it's a form of paying attention. If you listen to what is being said, and if you cross yourself because you mean it, and not just because everyone else is doing it, you're making that prayer your own."

"It becomes much more interesting when you get to adolescence, because you have to think it out for yourself."

"When I was little I was told that faith could move mountains. I didn't know it was just picture language. I thought it meant that if I believed something hard enough I could make a mountain move. We could see a mountain from our house, and I remember looking at the mountain and willing it to move! I decided that I didn't have enough faith.

It was only gradually, as I grew up, that I came to see that faith isn't about believing something impossible, it's about commitment, and about the way you put your Christian beliefs into practice in your life."

'An exact moment', 'a gradual process': interview people whose experience illustrates these different ways of growing up in Christianity.

Glossary

acolyte assistant as a communion service

Alternative Service Book Church of England prayer book introduced in 1980

chalice cup used for wine at communion

crucifix cross with figure of Jesus on it

deacon lay official in some Free Churches; also first of the three orders of the ordained ministry in Anglican and Roman Catholic Churches

denomination branch of the Christian Church

Ecumenical Councils gatherings representing the whole Christian Church in the first five centuries

epitaphius a painted figure of the dead Christ, representing his tomb

evensong service of evening prayer in the Anglican Church

extempore not prepared beforehand

iconostasis screen in Orthodox Church with icons painted on it

incense spice which produces a sweet smell when burnt

liturgy communion service

mass name for communion service, especially in the Roman Catholic Church

millennium period of a thousand years

paschal relating to Easter (and to the Jewish Passover)

passion 'suffering', the suffering of Christ on the cross

patriarchate region of the Orthodox Church headed by a Patriarch

puja worship (in Hinduism)

purgatory 'place' where souls were purified before entering heaven

rosary circle of beads used in prayer

venerate revere, give great respect to

vespers service of prayer for evenings

Index

NB Words in the index refer to where the topic is discussed and not only to where the actual words occur.

Advent 39, 42, 51
Africa 6, 9, 25–26, 30, 58
Anglican 4–6, 9–11, 15, 18, 20, 23, 34, 38, 41–42, 48, 61
Ascension 39, 42
Ash Wednesday 39, 41–42
baptism 4–10, 12, 15, 20, 31, 41–42, 47, 50
Baptist 6, 8–9, 16, 20
believers' baptism 8–9
Bible 10, 12, 20, 44–46, 50–54, 57, 60
bishop 6, 10–11, 15, 23
Brazil 40
calendar 38–39, 43
candles 4–5, 12, 25, 28, 30, 34–37, 39, 46, 50–51
choir 14, 23–24, 34–35
Christ 4–6, 10, 12–13, 16, 31–37, 56
Christmas 12, 20, 28, 30–31, 39, 42, 49, 55
communion 12, 14–19, 22, 35–36, 39, 41, 48
confession 18–19
confirmation 10–11, 15, 26
creeds 55–56
cross 4, 14, 26, 28, 32, 36, 41, 46, 56, 61
death 4, 36, 59
Easter 26, 28, 32–39, 41–42, 48, 51, 55
eggs 32–33
Epiphany 31, 39–40
eucharist (*see communion*)
fasting 16, 18–19, 36, 38–39, 41
festivals 14, 23, 26, 30–43, 47–48, 50–51
Germany 30–32, 40, 42
godparents 4, 6, 10, 50
Good Friday 20–21, 28, 36, 39, 41

Greek Orthodox 6, 12, 23–24, 33, 36–37
Holy Spirit 6, 10–11, 42, 55–57
Holy Week 35–36, 39, 41
icons 12–13, 16, 34–35, 37, 46–49, 57
India 25, 31
infant baptism 9–10
Jesus 8–9, 15–16, 28, 30–32, 35–36, 38–39, 41–42, 49–50, 52–53, 55–58, 60
Judaism 18, 30, 38, 55, 57
Lent 18, 20, 39–41
light 5, 12, 34–36, 46, 50–51
liturgy 12, 14, 23, 35, 37, 48, 61
marriage 4, 25
mass 12, 25, 32
Maundy Thursday 36, 39, 41
Methodist 11, 17
Mexico 4, 25
Mozambique 26
Orthodox Church 6, 12–13, 15–16, 18, 23–24, 28, 31–34, 39, 46–48, 55, 57
Palm Sunday 20, 35, 39, 41
paschal 34, 36–38
Pathfinders 50, 53
Pentecost 39, 42–43, 48
Pope 22–23, 38
prayer 10, 12, 18, 27–28, 36, 44–45, 47–48, 55, 57, 61
resurrection 34–36, 38
Roman Catholic 4, 10, 15–16, 18–19, 23, 25, 28, 34, 38, 41–42, 46, 48, 59
Russian Orthodox 14–15, 18, 23–24, 28, 30, 32, 34–35, 38, 55
saints 13, 26, 28, 43, 46–47, 55
Shrove Tuesday 20, 40
Sunday school 48, 50, 57

symbols 7, 9, 13, 31–32, 34, 36, 42, 56
Trinity 39, 42, 56–57
Tyndale 54
United Reformed 11
West Indian 14
Whitsun 20, 42, 50
Zimbabwe 26

Acknowledgements

We would like to express our very grateful thanks to the following, who helped by sharing their experiences of growing up in Christianity. Without them this book would not have been possible.

Isabel Antonio, Fernando Cervantes, Angela Enoch, Athene Hariades, Sharon Kirrane, Nicolas Lampe, Jane Lambert, Katie and Sophie Lowles, Hope, Luke and Naomi Price, Lisa von Schlippe, Adele Tapley, Jonathan and Nicola Webster.

We are also grateful to Fr Gary Cawthorne and Miss Constance Babbington-Smith for reading the manuscript.

We are grateful to the following for permission to reproduce photographs: Andes Press Agency, pages 11, 21 (photos: Carlos Reyes); Ateliers et Presse de Taize, page 27; Baptist Missionary Society, page 9; Barnaby's Picture Library, pages 32, 40; British Museum, page 52; Malcolm Clarke, page 34; Out Take (as appeared in *Greek Review*), page 37; Daisy Hayes, page 5; Iona Abbey, page 54; Lazarica Serbian Orthrodox Church of the Holy Prince Lazar, Birmingham, page 13; Mark Link, Society of Jesuits, page 56; Louise Pirouet, page 58; Popperfoto, page 22; Jamie Simson, page 29; Fellowship of St Albans and St Sergius, page 47; John Twinning, pages 7, 19, 51, 61; United Society for the Propagation of the Gospel, page 31; Geoff Ward, pages 15, 17, 45, 49. Photographs on pages 25 and 43, supplied by the authors.
Cover: Candles being lit in Notre Dame, Paris (Photo: Picturepoint Ltd).

LONGMAN GROUP LIMITED,
Edinburgh Gate, Harlow,
Essex, CM20 2JE
and Associated Companies throughout the world.

© Longman Group UK Limited 1990

First published 1990
Third impression 1995

Set in 12/14pt Palatino
Printed in Hong Kong
NPC/03

ISBN 0 582 00283 4